CATHOLIC COLLEGES
AND
FEDERAL FUNDING

CATHOLIC COLLEGES
AND
FEDERAL FUNDING

By

K. D. WHITEHEAD
Deputy Assistant Secretary for
Higher Education Programs
U.S. Department of Education

IGNATIUS PRESS   SAN FRANCISCO

Cover by Roxanne Mei Lum

© 1988 Ignatius Press, San Francisco
ISBN 0-89870-187-2
Library of Congress catalogue number 87-82979
Printed in the United States of America

To
Bill and Onalee McGraw

Contents

8   *Contents*

Foreword

In *Crisis* magazine of March 1987, an article of mine appeared which attacked, as a "sham and a shame" the claim of the presidents of 110 colleges of "Catholic" identity that they were forced to secularize in order to obtain public funding. They had joined in a public renunciation of a draft proposal by the Vatican pointing to a definition of an institution of higher education which can properly and worthily bear the name "Catholic". While my short article was not intended as a legal brief pinpointing the errors in the positions of the 110, now such a brief is at hand, and I am honored to write its preface. Kenneth D. Whitehead is amply qualified to speak in detail to the issue raised. Named Deputy Assistant Secretary for Higher Education Programs by U.S. Education Secretary William J. Bennett in 1986, he had previously served four years as the department's Director of International Education Programs.

A particularly unfortunate aspect of the colleges' public reliance upon the "loss of funding" pretext has been the influencing of some Church leaders by this unfounded claim. Hence there have been statements by some in high positions agreeing, in effect, that no attempt should be made to reprove the "Catholic" colleges for their lack of fidelity, since, if the colleges re-Catholicized, they would be doomed to go under financially. If these Church officials were really taken in by the "loss of funding" plea, Mr. Whitehead's book leaves them with no recourse but to face the facts. These are two: (1) that the loss of funding argument is false and (2) that, regardless of "controversy", the mind of the Church must be spoken with unmistakable clarity.

William Bentley Ball

I

"Institutional Autonomy" and "Academic Freedom": Essential for Federal Aid to Higher Education?

In January 1987, Father Charles E. Curran was suspended from his position as a professor of theology at the Catholic University of America by Archbishop of Washington James A. Hickey, acting in his capacity as university chancellor. Father Curran at first threatened to defy the suspension and to show up to teach his classes anyway. "As a tenured professor, I have a legally binding contract", he told a press conference. "The question is, can an external authority break that contract?"[1]

Father Curran evidently considered the university's chancellor, who is also the archbishop of Washington, to be somehow "external" to the university itself, thus providing grounds for him to challenge his suspension as having been imposed from "outside". "Obviously it's a lawyer's dream", he declared confidently.

In the event, however, Father Curran did not

[1] *Chronicle of Higher Education,* Jan. 21, 1987.

show up to teach his classes after all. His stated reason for not doing so, in addition to his concern for not involving his students in his dispute with university and ecclesiastical authorities, turned out to be most interesting. As Father Curran explained to a press conference, Archbishop Hickey had responded to Father Curran's threat to ignore his suspension by the archbishop by threatening in turn to invoke a provision of Catholic Canon Law prescribing that "those who teach theological subjects in any institute of higher studies must have a mandate from the competent ecclesiastical authority" (Canon 812). This canon, included in the new Code of Canon Law promulgated in 1983, had never been invoked in the United States. According to Father Curran, its invoking by the archbishop would have posed a danger generally to "the academic freedom and autonomy" of Catholic colleges and universities and "would have serious consequences for academic accreditation, government funding, and a host of other issues important to Catholic higher education in the United States".[2] Father Curran averred that he did not want to be responsible for the far-reaching precedent that would have been established by Archbishop Hickey's having

[2] Ibid.

recourse to Canon 812, and he therefore drew back. "If there is a story today, the story is that Curran blinked", he said, to the applause of many of his supporters present at his press conference.[3]

The position adopted by Father Curran on this occasion has been a common one in Catholic higher education circles. Leaders in Catholic higher education have generally taken to holding that what they call "institutional autonomy" and "academic freedom" are both essential to their survival—essential because they are apparently thought to be requisites for receiving government aid. On an earlier occasion, Father Curran more fully explained the general position, which he holds in common with many of the leaders of Catholic higher education today:

Catholic colleges and universities receive a large amount of financial help in different forms from the public monies of the state. In the past, the Supreme Court has ruled such public funding is acceptable for Catholic higher education but not for Catholic elementary and high schools. The difference between higher and lower education is that in higher education there is no indoctrination and the principles of academic freedom are observed. Thus, if there

[3] *New York Times,* Jan. 16, 1987.

were no academic freedom and institutional autonomy for Catholic higher education, it might very well be that the court would rule that public funding for Catholic institutions of higher learning is unconstitutional".[4]

Basing one's educational policy on what the United States Supreme Court might do in the future seems to be a rather unusual way for any educational enterprise sure of its own character and aims to proceed. If Father Curran showed the same respect for the decisions of his own Church that he shows for the hypothetical future decisions of the United States Supreme Court, it is unlikely that he would be having the same difficulties with the authorities of his Church that he in fact appears to be having. However that may be, the general position spelled out here by Father Curran appears to be widely held, if not indeed nearly universally held, by the leaders of Catholic higher education in the United States today.

The Association of Catholic Colleges and Universities (ACCU), for example, responding in February 1986 to a "Proposed Schema for a Pontifical Document on Catholic Universities" circulated by the Congregation for Catholic Ed-

[4] Charles E. Curran, "On Dissent in the Church", *Commonweal*, Sept. 12, 1986, p. 470.

ucation in Rome, took substantially the same position as Father Curran. In a synthesis of responses to Rome from 110 Catholic college and university presidents prepared by Sister Alice Gallin, O.S.U., executive director of the ACCU, the organization assured the Vatican Congregation for Catholic Education that

> [t]he present reality of government funding to students attending Catholic colleges and universities and the eligibility of our institutions for direct grants for research or construction is a very complex issue, one which needs to be understood by those who think we exaggerate the problems that would result from the imposition of external ecclesiastical control.

According to Sister Gallin in this ACCU synthesis:

> Catholic institutions . . . must meet the standards for accreditation by regional accrediting agencies recognized by civil authorities . . . such accreditation, as well as the federal and state funding that accompanies it, requires that institutions respect academic freedom and that the curriculum not be used for proselytizing on behalf of any religion.

Sister Gallin cited two Supreme Court decisions that, in her view, clearly required institutional autonomy and academic freedom as a condition of government aid. She concluded that "it is virtually *certain* that such aid would be withdrawn" (emphasis added) if it could ever be shown that Catholic colleges and universities were "controlled" by the Catholic Church.[5]

This conclusion might appear surprising to the average person, who probably assumes that churches or other sponsoring bodies in a free and pluralistic society can and ought to be able to exercise at least some degree of control over the educational institutions they sponsor. Most religiously affiliated colleges in the United States were founded to provide a higher education in accordance with the tenets and spirit of their sponsoring churches. Many Catholic colleges and universities were similarly erected with the gifts poor immigrants made for that very purpose, and many of them have functioned, fully accredited, for many decades while providing a quality higher education in an authentic Catholic religious context. It is not clear what claim Catholic or similarly religiously affiliated schools would continue to have on the support of their church communities if they now suddenly "are, and of right ought to be, free and indepen-

[5] "Catholic College and University Presidents Respond to Proposed Vatican Schema", *Origins: NC Documentary Service*, vol. 15, no. 43, Apr. 10, 1986, pp. 699–700.

dent",[6] as some leaders of Catholic education now seem to be claiming.

For this *is* the position being advanced by many of the leaders of Catholic higher education today. This is what they are telling the Catholic bishops; this is what they are telling the Congregation for Catholic Education in Rome. They claim that "institutional autonomy" and "academic freedom" are essential for accreditation—and accreditation is in turn, according to them, a requirement for any government aid. Father Theodore M. Hesburgh, long the president of Notre Dame University, told the *New York Times:* "We would stand to lose a lot of government assistance if we conformed to the dictates of the church. Parochial schools cannot get government assistance because they are an arm of the church. Notre Dame and other Catholic universities can get assistance because we are free and autonomous."[7] Father Hesburgh has elsewhere flatly asserted: "Institutional autonomy is essential to federal support."[8] And federal support, of course, is considered essential to institutional survival. No

[6] The Declaration of Independence, July 4, 1776.

[7] *New York Times,* Nov. 16, 1986.

[8] Theodore M. Hesburgh, C.S.C., "Catholic Education in America", *America*, Oct. 4, 1986, p. 163.

doubt because of Father Hesburgh's promi-
nence, this particular statement of his has been
widely disseminated.[9] If true, it would certainly
provide one explanation for the rush on the part
of so many Catholic colleges and universities in
America to secularize themselves over the past
two decades. But is it true?

Father Charles E. Curran certainly thinks so.
He felt constrained to draw back, once it became
a question of implementing for the first time in
America a provision of Catholic Canon Law that
would have unequivocally demonstrated the ul-
timate authority of the archbishop of Washington over the Department of Theology of the
Catholic University of America.

Of course, it is true that Father Curran subsequently filed suit against the university to over-
turn his suspension—on the grounds that the
university violated his contract.[10] But he was
clearly unwilling, from his perspective, to put
the entire Catholic higher education enterprise
at risk by being the occasion of a demonstration

[9] Ari L. Goldman, "Catholic Colleges in U.S. Debate
Academic Freedom amid Disputes", *New York Times*, Oct. 8,
1986; see also Peter Hebblethwaite, "Baum Unlikely Medi-
ator between U.S. and Vatican", *National Catholic Reporter,*
Jan. 23, 1987.

[10] *New York Times,* March 3, 1987.

that the Catholic Church is, in fact, able to "control" its own schools with respect to the "theological subjects" taught there.

Government aid has come to be considered far too important for that. It is certainly clear that the need for government aid can provide a convenient pretext for any group of religiously affiliated schools wishing to claim autonomy from their sponsoring church.

Even some of the Catholic educators who specifically eschew accepting any government funding appear to be doing so because they too believe that accepting such government funding would require them to sever their organic lines with the Catholic Church.[11]

What is the truth of the matter?

[11] See the news story on the decision of Christendom College in Front Royal, Virginia, not to accept government funding even in the form of student financial assistance: *Washington Times*, Feb. 20, 1987.

II

Eligibility Requirements
for Federal Aid

What are the eligibility requirements for receiving federal aid for higher education? Can religiously affiliated colleges and universities receive it? Before these questions can be answered properly, a number of preliminary observations must be made.

First, the focus of this inquiry will be on federal aid, both because of its importance and because it is easier to cover the entire issue of government aid to higher education by concentrating on the federal level. It is true that some states have been more restrictive in according financial aid to religiously affiliated colleges and universities than the federal government has been, but this is not true of all or even a majority of the states; by and large the assumptions and practices of the states in providing aid to higher education tend to reflect those of the federal government. Moreover, by far the larger share of government aid that goes to private institutions, such as those with religious affiliations, is from federal rather than state or

21

local sources. Once we have delineated eligibility requirements for federal aid, we may then make some mention of state aid as well.

Second, even where federal aid is concerned, a distinction must be made between the requirements of civil rights statutes and those statutes that specifically authorize various types of aid. All institutions benefiting from any kind of federal support are required to observe the civil rights laws of the United States. Some of the implications of this must be examined further on. Certainly the "institutional autonomy" and "academic freedom" of all American institutions of higher learning vis-à-vis the federal government have been profoundly affected by the civil rights revolution of the past three decades.

Third, this inquiry is concerned only with government institutional and student aid, not with federal research grants in various, mostly scientific, fields. The church-state issue scarcely enters into this latter type of government research aid at all, except where a religiously affiliated school, for example, because of its particular tenets might decline to engage in certain types of medical research, much as wholly secular schools or professors might decline to engage in, say, defense-related research.

Fourth, the situation regarding federal aid to religiously affiliated institutions of higher education is quite different from the situation regarding federal or state aid of almost any kind to religious schools on the elementary and secondary levels. Under current Supreme Court interpretations of the First Amendment, which prohibits any "establishment of religion", direct government aid to religious schools since the 1940s has been held to be an instance of such an "establishment of religion". This has been true to the point where, currently, no federal aid, and generally speaking no public aid at all, can flow to religious schools on the elementary and secondary levels for general operating purposes. Later on it will be necessary to look briefly at some of the Supreme Court decisions that have equated government aid to religious schools as an "establishment of religion"; to some extent, government aid to higher education has also been affected by these court decisions. But the simple historical fact is that substantial government aid has long flowed both to religiously affiliated colleges and, especially, to students in such colleges, without serious First Amendment questions ever having been raised about the greater part of this aid. The Supreme Court decisions that affect higher education date only from the 1970s—that is, after government aid had already been flowing to religiously affiliated colleges, especially in the form of the student financial aid, for decades.

Father Charles E. Curran was quoted above as

explaining this historical fact by declaring that "the difference between higher and lower education is that in higher education there is no indoctrination and the principles of academic freedom are observed". Sister Alice Gallin was similarly quoted above as holding that "federal and state funding . . . requires that institutions respect academic freedom and that the curriculum not be used for proselytizing on behalf of any religion." It will be necessary to examine whether and to what extent these assertions are true. What can be stated at the outset, however, is that both of these statements are simplifications of the real situation.

What is much more pertinent to the fact that government aid of all types has been accorded much more freely to religiously affiliated higher education institutions than to religious schools on the elementary and secondary levels, however, is the undoubted historical fact that, in marked contrast to the system of public schools on the lower levels, higher education in the United States literally began under religious sponsorship—Harvard, Yale, and Princeton were all religiously affiliated in the beginning—and these and similar schools were already well established before the states ever seriously got into the business of sponsoring state colleges and universities. At the time the First Amendment was enacted, most higher education in the United States was being carried out by religiously affiliated colleges. Even today, the number of private as opposed to state-sponsored colleges and universities constitutes a significant portion of the total U.S. higher education enterprise. And the percentage of private higher education institutions that still retain religious affiliation similarly remains high even at a time when trends toward secularization are strong.

Of the approximately thirty-three hundred institutions of higher education in the United States, over seventeen hundred, or more than half, are "independent", that is, not primarily state supported; of these seventeen hundred private schools, more than eight hundred, or nearly half, are religiously affiliated (Catholic colleges and universities currently number between 230 and 235).[1]

By contrast, less than one-fifth of the elementary and secondary schools in the United States are private schools.[2] The much higher portion of the total U.S. higher education universe oc-

[1] *Digest of Education Statistics, 1983–84,* 21st ed. (National Center for Education Statistics, U.S. Department of Education, U.S. Government Printing Office, Washington, D.C. 20402), pp. 104–5.
[2] Ibid., p. 12.

cupied by private and religiously affiliated colleges and universities points to the practical difficulty of ever building the same kind of "wall of separation" across higher education that the Supreme Court has in fact succeeded in erecting across elementary and secondary education. To have tried to establish the same First Amendment prohibitions against any government aid to private or religiously affiliated colleges and universities as have been established against government aid to religious schools at lower levels would have meant, quite simply, excluding a significant percentage of higher education institutions from any government aid. Even the Supreme Court has prudently avoided going as far as that. The outcry from the cities, counties, and states where the more than half of all colleges that would be cut off from government aid are located can well be imagined.

One of the other consequences of the fact that so much of U.S. higher education remains in private hands is that colleges and universities themselves largely determine their own nature, statutes, and curriculum. They were already doing this long before the individual states ever got into the business of higher education, and certainly before federal aid to education was ever dreamed of. There is no national "ministry of education" in the United States. The very statute by which the federal Department of Education was eventually established (in 1979!) prohibits the Secretary of Education from prescribing educational curricula at any level or interfering with "academic freedom". The most significant exception to this governmental non-interference has come through the enforcement of federal civil rights statutes. The American education system is nevertheless still one of the freest in the world. As Terry W. Hartle, formerly of the American Enterprise Institute and now an adviser to the Senate Committee on Labor and Human Resources, recently observed: "Colleges have enormous autonomy in governing their internal affairs. Almost no other social institution has the freedom to fix its own agenda that we give to higher education. Who teaches what to whom and how they teach it are, for the most part, still matters that are settled on the campus."[3]

Or, it might be added, off the campus as well, if that is the choice of the school, for one of the further consequences of this same freedom of the American education system is that churches or other groups can set up and operate their own colleges in accordance with their own tenets

[3] Terry W. Hartle, "Is It Really 'Higher' Education?" *Washington Post*, Oct. 23, 1986.

and requirements. Nothing prohibits them from doing so; the federal government does not get involved at all in such decisions, and state requirements are generally limited to the broadest and most general types of questions that apply impartially to all. As the Supreme Court decided more than a century ago: "The right to organize voluntary religious associations . . . is unquestioned. But it would . . . lead to the total subversion of such religious bodies if anyone aggrieved by one of their decisions could appeal to the secular courts and have them reversed."[4]

Religiously affiliated colleges can qualify for most kinds of state and federal aid to higher education. Existing direct prohibitions of federal aid to religiously affiliated schools are minimal. Divinity schools or schools of theology are generally not eligible for direct federal aid (although *students* in these institutions can and often do receive general student financial assistance). Sometimes this divinity school prohibition is specifically mentioned in the program authorization, as in Titles III and VII of the Higher Education Act of 1965. Sometimes divinity students are excluded from federally supported graduate fellowships, as in Title IX of the same law. This is believed to be consistent with

[4] *Watson* v. *Jones*, 80 U.S. 679 (1871).

the First Amendment prohibition of the "estab-lishment of religion" in the broadest sense, but it is surely minimal as far as the total amount of aid is concerned.

The question, though, is whether religiously affiliated colleges and universities can qualify generally for various types of federal assistance to higher education, and the answer is emphati-cally "yes". First of all, by far the larger part of total federal aid to higher education flows, at least in theory, directly to *students* in the form of federal student financial assistance—grants, loans, work-study programs, and the like. This type of federal student financial assistance goes back to World War II's GI Bill of Rights. Hun-dreds of thousands of veterans gained access to higher education as a result of this pioneering legislation. No distinction was made about the possible religious character, if any, of the thou-sands of colleges and universities attended by veterans under the GI Bill. As one study de-scribed the situation: "There was virtually no process for supervision over which institutions veterans could attend."[5]

Since there was no direct support of "religion"

[5] Charles M. Chambers, "Federal Government and Ac-creditation", in Kenneth E. Young, Charles M. Chambers, H. R. Kells, and Associates, *Understanding Accreditation* (San Francisco: Jossey-Bass, 1983), p. 239.

as distinguished from "education" (which nevertheless could be imparted in a total religious context, and was so imparted in hundreds of religiously affiliated schools under the GI Bill), no serious First Amendment problem ever arose. The Higher Education Act of 1965, under which most types of federal aid to higher education are authorized today, similarly did not and does not discriminate against religiously affiliated schools except where divinity schools or students are specifically excluded from specific institutional aid programs.

However, federal student financial assistance, which in theory flows directly to students, is now in fact largely administered by the educational institutions themselves through their financial aid offices. In order for a student to be eligible for federal student financial assistance, therefore, the institution in which he is enrolled must itself be *eligible* for federal aid. The same thing is true for the various types of federal institutional assistance that exist—much smaller in money terms than student financial assistance, by the way: in 1986 less than $500 million annually in federal institutional aid was disbursed, compared to more than $8 billion in total federal student financial assistance.[6] In other words,

[6] *The Fiscal Year 1988 Budget* (U.S. Department of Edu-

more than 93 percent of all the federal aid to education consists of financial assistance going directly to students and distributed without regard to the religious affiliation, if any, of the schools the students attend.

The question now becomes, for institutional aid as well as for student financial assistance: What are the eligibility requirements for receiving this aid? This is the question posed at the beginning of this chapter. What is the answer?

Section 1201 of the Higher Education Act of 1965 specifies which higher education institutions are eligible for federal aid by the simple expedient of defining what it means by an institution of higher education. According to the definition in the law, the institution must be located in a U.S. state or territory; it must admit students, with high school diplomas or their equivalent, or else students beyond the age of compulsory school attendance with the "ability to benefit"; it must be legally authorized by the state or territory in which it is located to provide a program of education beyond the secondary level; and it must either award a bachelor's degree or provide at least a two-year program of classes with credits that count toward a bach-

cation, 400 Maryland Avenue SW, Washington, D.C. 20202), pp. 9–11.

elor's degree. (Other sections of the act expand these provisions of Section 1201 in ways that make students in vocational education programs or those in wholly privately owned proprietary schools, such as barber colleges and beauty schools, also eligible for federal student financial assistance.)

Finally—and this is the key provision in the Higher Education Act's definition of an institution of higher education—the institution must be "accredited". By accreditation the Higher Education Act specifies either full accreditation by a nationally recognized accrediting agency, or else the attainment of a preaccreditation status looking toward such full accreditation.

Since some private institutions in the pluralistic American system of higher education, especially some religiously affiliated institutions, have traditionally and for their own reasons declined even to present themselves for accreditation to accrediting agencies, the law provides for a special type of accreditation. Those unaccredited schools whose credits are accepted on transfer by other institutions that are regularly accredited are themselves considered accredited for purposes of federal aid. Far from threatening religiously affiliated colleges with ineligibility for federal assistance if they do not wish to be regularly accredited, then, Congress clearly went out of its way in this law to ensure that eligibility for federal aid to higher education would be as wide as the diversity of U.S. higher education itself. Even schools that do not wish to seek formal accreditation can be considered accredited for purposes of receiving federal aid if their credits are accepted by other accredited schools.

It should be noted that nowhere in these requirements for eligibility for federal aid is there any mention of "institutional autonomy" or "academic freedom", the lack of which, according to Sister Alice Gallin of the ACCU, was supposed to lead to *certain* withdrawal of federal aid to Catholic colleges and universities. The fact is that these two things are not requirements for federal financial assistance; accreditation, however, is a requirement. Are "institutional autonomy" and "academic freedom" required for accreditation? This is the question that needs to be examined next.

III

Accreditation Requirements for Higher Educational Institutions

One of the venerable and distinctive features of the American system of higher education is that the maintenance of educational standards is not the responsibility of the government but rather of private, voluntary associations called accrediting agencies. Colleges and universities are accredited by these accrediting agencies only when they reach and maintain certain standards of performance, quality, and integrity. By requiring that schools generally be accredited by an agency recognized by the Secretary of Education as the principal condition of eligibility for federal aid, the federal government is endorsing the standards and criteria of these private, voluntary accrediting agencies rather than establishing standards, criteria, or other requirements of its own.

According to the Council on Postsecondary Accreditation, the aims of accreditation are to:

— foster excellence through the development of uniform national criteria and guidelines for assessing educational effectiveness;

— encourage improvement through continuous self-study and review;
— assure the educational community, the public, and other interested agencies or organizations that an educational institution or program has clearly defined and appropriate objectives and maintains conditions in which these objectives can be and are being carried out;
— provide assistance and counsel to both established and developing institutions and programs; and
— endeavor to protect institutions against encroachments that might jeopardize their educational effectiveness or academic freedom.[1]

As can be seen from this summary of its principal aims, accreditation is primarily a matter of educational "quality control". It is not immediately evident from this summary, however, that "institutional autonomy" and "academic freedom" are requirements for accreditation. Only the last of the aims enumerated here even mentions "academic freedom". And "institu-

[1] In *The Balance Wheel for Accreditation*, Annual Directory (The Council on Postsecondary Accreditation, 1 Dupont Circle NW, Suite 305, Washington, D.C. 20036, July 1986), p. 3.

tional autonomy", as such, is not mentioned in this summary of the aims of accreditation at all, although the Council on Postsecondary Accreditation elsewhere does include, in its "Provision for Recognition", a mention of the development of "evaluative criteria to allow and encourage institutional freedom and autonomy".[2]

Thus "institutional autonomy" and "academic freedom" in the most general sense are indeed included among the characteristics expected of higher education. However, side by side with its mention of the development and encouragement of "institutional autonomy", the Council on Postsecondary Accreditation also declares that accreditation agencies should recognize "the right of institutions or programs to be evaluated in *the light of their own stated purposes* so long as these are consistent with purposes generally recognized by the postsecondary education community" (emphasis added).[3] In other words, if the stated purpose of a religiously affiliated college or university is to provide a higher edu-

---

[2] *Provisions and Procedures for Becoming Recognized as an Accrediting Body for Postsecondary Educational Institutions or Programs* (The Council on Postsecondary Accreditation, July 1986), p. 3.

[3] Ibid.

cation within the specific context of the teachings of a given religion or denomination, carrying out this stated purpose would in no way constitute a bar to accreditation; the institution is nowhere required to meet some abstract definition of "academic freedom" or "institutional autonomy" imposed from outside in order to be accredited. On the contrary, the institution is allowed to set forth its own stated purposes by which it is to be judged. And, in fact, it has been the traditional practice in America to accredit religiously affiliated institutions on their own terms, provided educational standards are maintained.

If one looks at the requirements of the major accrediting agencies, it turns out that the right of institutions to function within the framework of their own stated purposes is indeed recognized. Institutional integrity and autonomy are encouraged as important values in authentic higher education, but they are in no way absolute. The Northwest Association of Schools and Colleges, for example, calls for "institutional integrity" in the way a college or university manages its affairs—"specifies its goals, selects and retains its faculty, admits students, establishes curricula, determines programs of research, fixes its fields of service".[4] Again, however, this is not

[4] *Accreditation Handbook,* 1984 edition (Northwest Asso-

absolute, since this particular agency, like the other accrediting agencies, regularly accredits state universities or community colleges that are, ultimately, under the total control of state or local governments. (The same thing is true, of course, in the so-called proprietary school sector, where wholly owned and controlled institutions, which are "independent" in no sense at all, are regularly accredited, thus enabling their students to become the beneficiaries of enormous amounts of federal student financial assistance.)

As for academic freedom, the Northwest Agency declares that those within institutions of higher learning must have as their "first concern evidence of truth rather than particular judgments of institutional benefactors, concerns of churchmen, public opinion, social pressure, or political proscription". At the same time, the Northwest Association specifically affirms that "intellectual freedom does not rule out commitment. . . . Institutions may hold to a particular political, social, or religious philosophy."[5] This is an important qualification, since the position of the Catholic educators under discussion seems

ciation of Schools and Colleges, Commission on Colleges, 3700B University Way NE, Seattle, Washington 98105), p. 91.

[5] Ibid., p. 92.

to be that an American institution of higher learning cannot include real commitment to a specific religious doctrine; this does not appear to be the view of this typical accrediting association. What the association does require, though, is that an institution "publish candidly any reasonable limitations on freedom of inquiry or expression which are dictated by institutional purposes".[6]

In other words, a religiously affiliated institution requiring a certain standard of doctrinal "orthodoxy" on the part of its faculty, for example, would *not* jeopardize its accreditation, provided it plainly announces beforehand its requirements in this regard. In practice, the same thing would be true of requirements regarding the moral behavior expected of faculty members or students at the institution.

The various U.S. accrediting agencies are remarkably similar in their requirements. The *Accreditation Handbook* of the Northwest Association of Schools and Colleges, which has been consulted here to establish general accreditation criteria with regard to "institutional autonomy" and "academic freedom", is similar to the publications that each of the major accrediting agencies publishes for the same purpose. In another

[6] Ibid., p. 89.

publication entitled *Criteria for Accreditation,* for example, the Southern Association of Colleges and Schools sees the purpose of accreditation primarily as the maintenance of educational quality; the agency "supports the right of an institution to pursue its established educational purpose". Within this framework it too includes "academic freedom" among the desired characteristics of a higher education, and is especially concerned with "institutional autonomy" in that it requires each institution to have its own distinct legal governing board, which is "the legal body responsible for the institution". However, the Southern Association sees this governing board not as totally autonomous and without organic links to any external sponsor; rather, it expressly declares that the governing board "*represents* the interests of the founders, *the supporting religious group,* the supporting governmental agency, or other supporting party" (emphasis added).[7]

Far from being entirely free, autonomous, and independent, then, American institutions of higher education typically do have organic

[7] *Criteria for Accreditation* (Commission on Colleges, Southern Association of Colleges and Schools, 795 Peachtree Street NE, Atlanta, Georgia 30365, 1984), pp. 5, 26.

links of dependency with elements within the larger community beyond the campus. Private institutions are often thus linked to a sponsoring body, which may be a church, just as state institutions are linked to and ultimately dependent on the state government. A review of the published accrediting standards of American accrediting agencies quickly reveals that the freedom and diversity of the American system of higher education in this regard are consistently respected. Institutions are free to set themselves up and function according to goals and standards that they have largely set for themselves, provided educational quality is maintained, just as church and state authorities are also able to set them up and operate them in accordance with declared principles.

The conclusion is inescapable: "institutional autonomy" and "academic freedom" are defined to permit wide variations in practice. They clearly allow for institutional freedom of religion. Narrowly defined as the freedom of professors to teach what they want, or as the freedom of an institution to be free of any constraints from its sponsoring church or other body, they are clearly *not* requirements for accreditation (and hence for federal aid).

However, because the whole issue of "academic freedom" has been further represented as meaning that religious "indoctrination" cannot take place in accredited institutions of higher education (Father Curran), or that the curriculum cannot "be used for proselytizing" (Sister Gallin), or that a college may not be "an arm of the church" (Father Hesburgh), it is necessary that the issue of academic freedom as it is actually understood and practiced in America be examined further. Could a religiously affiliated institution accused or convicted of "indoctrination" or "proselytizing" conceivably lose its accreditation and hence its eligibility for federal aid? This question is especially important because it is also related to what the Supreme Court has styled "excessive government entanglement with religion", a topic that must also be examined further on. But first it is necessary to look more closely at "academic freedom" as it is actually understood and practiced in the United States.

IV

Academic Freedom in Theory and Practice

"Academic freedom" is generally understood to refer to the freedom of academic faculty members to search for truth in accordance with the canons of their particular scholarly disciplines and to expound the results of this search for truth without undue restrictions being placed on them by university or outside authorities, or, more especially, without jeopardizing their academic positions and their tenure in these positions. The freedom of churches or other groups to set up, operate, and control without restriction their own colleges and universities—or, for example, what ought properly to be the equal freedom of students and their parents to be assured that a higher education advertised as being imparted within a particular religious context will in fact be authentically such—these important freedoms are scarcely ever even mentioned in connection with the subject of academic freedom.

It is as if the freedom of university professors were somehow greater or more absolute that the freedom of citizens or other social institutions generally; or as if, as George Orwell put it in *Animal Farm,* some animals were "more equal than others". This would be a hard thesis to defend. Usually no attempt is made to defend it; it is simply assumed. Any fair appraisal of the proper place of the professor's freedom within academia, however, clearly has to be balanced against the rights of sponsoring institutions to ensure that their tenets are observed and the rights of students and parents to be assured that the education imparted in any given institution accords with what is advertised as the purpose of that institution.

The most common definition of academic freedom, usually cited wherever the question is discussed, is that of the philosopher Arthur O. Lovejoy in the *Encyclopedia of the Social Sciences:*

> Academic freedom is the freedom of the teacher or research worker in higher institutions of learning to investigate and discuss the problems of his science and to express his conclusions, whether through publication or in the instruction of students, *without interference from political or ecclesiastical authority,* or the administrative officials of the institution in which he is employed, unless his methods are found by qualified bodies of his own profession to be

clearly incompetent or contrary to professional
ethics [emphasis added].[1]

It will be immediately apparent that this definition of academic freedom simply absolutizes
the right of the professor. Do institutions themselves have no rights? Does society have no rights
vis-à-vis its learned institutions? Do professors
not have any *responsibility* to "political or ecclesiastical authority" as the duly constituted voices
of the particular communities they serve?
Nothing of the kind could ever be guessed from
the above definition.

With respect to the question of religiously
affiliated colleges and universities, where any
exercise of purely religious authority might be
deemed a violation of some professor's rights
under the above definition, two further observations need to be made: (1) the kind of "academic
freedom" being set up for emulation here has
never existed in America in pure form, even in
secular institutions; and (2) standards commonly accepted in the American tradition of
higher education have never required religiously affiliated institutions to accord such an

[1] Arthur O. Lovejoy, "Academic Freedom", in *Encyclopedia of the Social Sciences*, edited by Edwin R. A. Seligmon and
Alvin Johnson (New York: Macmillan, 1980), p. 384.

unlimited degree of professional autonomy but rather have specifically held that colleges have the right to expect the professors employed by them to be willing to accept certain limitations. Each of these two points deserves some elaboration.

With respect to the degree to which "academic freedom" as defined by Lovejoy and invoked by those who wish to be free of constraints on what they may teach or publish is a reality in higher education in the United States today, it is worth reviewing what a major observer of the American higher education scene has recently written on this subject. In *Academic Strategy: The Management Revolution in American Higher Education*,[2] George Keller has styled as simply a "myth" the idea that "each college or university is close to an Athenian democracy of professional scholars who know each other and share a bundle of values and aspirations, which they practice in their institutional lives". According to Keller, it is equally a "myth" that "there was once an Edenic time in U.S. history when a condition of faculty control and Athenian self-government did exist". Not so, Keller writes: "Throughout most of

[2] George Keller, *Academic Strategy: The Management Revolution in America Higher Education.* (Baltimore and London: Johns Hopkins University Press, 1983).

the history of higher education, clergymen, politicians, merchants, pedagogical entrepreneurs and autocratic presidents have run the colleges, often with a stern grip."

Historically, threats to academic freedom regularly "came from imperious presidents, trustees, and state governors".[3] Since the civil rights legislation of the 1960s and 1970s, one has to add the federal government to this list as well. More than that, according to Keller:

> There is also the reality that some kinds of colleges—most two-year community colleges and predominantly black institutions, many church-affiliated colleges, and a large portion of the former teachers' colleges that are now State colleges—have seldom practiced faculty governance and still do not. While the ideology of faculty control pertains to all U.S. professors, the reality is that perhaps one-third of all faculty members exercise control of the academic sector.[4]

It would be tempting to pursue further Keller's treatment of academic freedom. He points out, for example, that the idea of academic freedom as claimed by American academics

[3] Ibid., pp. 30–31, 33–34.
[4] Ibid., p. 37.

goes back to the supposed academic freedom and self-governance of the venerable British universities and also to that symbolized by what was called *Lehrfreiheit* in the German universities of the nineteenth century. Yet the reality is that both Oxford and Cambridge "were compelled to submit in the 1870s to reforms suggested by a royal commission and enforced by parliamentary decrees"; and

> [W]hile German universities appeared to be academically free, they were actually run by the education ministers of each state. The professors were considered civil servants, and academic freedom was gained only by avoiding political and social issues and matters sensitive to the Prussian and local leaders.[5]

There is no intention here to belittle the value of academic freedom by the recital of such facts as these. Academic freedom clearly is, and ought to be, a treasured value in the American or any other system of higher education, a value to be appropriately respected and defended. Indeed, as will emerge later on, the threat posed to academic and some other kinds of freedom by certain misguided directions being taken in the enforcement of federal civil rights laws is cur-

[5] Ibid., p. 32.

rently very real, and those directions need to be resisted by all types of institutions, religiously affiliated or not.

However, when an attempt is made to absolutize the right of professors to teach what they please, even at the expense of other important values, it is necessary to recall that academic freedom has in fact never occupied quite the absolute place that is sometimes claimed for it; nor are supposed violations of it by church officials quite as shocking and heinous as they are sometimes made to appear by comparison with strictly secular academic models and practice. The fact is that there are definite limits to what typical U.S. universities will tolerate in the way of professorial behavior and opinion; for example, it is a safe bet that no U.S. institution today would tolerate the theory or practice of white supremacy in the name of academic freedom. During the campus turmoil of the sixties and seventies, faculty members, including some with tenure, were dismissed outright by prestigious secular universities.[6]

Furthermore it is a fact that current typical case law, in cases of conflict between universities and faculty members, generally recognizes that

[6] Diane Ravitch, *The Troubled Crusade: American Education, 1945–1980* (New York: Basic Books, 1983), chapter V.

academic freedom applies more fundamentally to institutions than to the claimed rights of professors to say whatever they think. In such cases of conflict, a recent law review writer has concluded that "the institution will almost always prevail".[7]

With regard to religiously affiliated institutions, it has in any case never been customary in higher education in the United States to require that academic freedom take precedence over specifically religious goals and teachings. The most commonly accepted formulation of what is expected of academic institutions in according academic freedom to their faculty is contained in the 1940 *Statement of Principles on Academic Freedom and Tenure* adopted and promulgated by the American Association of University Professors and, up to now, endorsed by some 120 academic associations.[8] This *Statement*, predictably, calls

[7] Kathryn D. Katz, "The First Amendment's Protection of Expressive Activity in the University Classroom: A Constitutional Myth", *Law Journal*, University of California (Davis), vol. 16, 1983, p. 859. Quoted by Msgr. George A. Kelly, "Academic Freedom for the Catholic College", *Fellowship of Catholic Scholars Newsletter*, Sept. 1987, p. 11.

[8] *Statement of Principles on Academic Freedom and Tenure*, adopted in 1940 by the American Association of University Professors, 1012 Fourteenth Street NW, Suite 500, Washington, D.C. 20005.

for "freedom for the teacher in research and in
the publication of the results" and also "in the
classroom in discussing his subject". But the
Statement quite explicitly includes an exception
for religion by affiliated institutions, as follows:
"Limitations of academic freedom because of
religious or other aims of the institution should
be clearly stated in writing at the time of the
appointment." There is no ambiguity in this
sentence at all; the right of religious institutions
to establish their own standards is recognized.

However, in 1970 the AAUP adopted some
further "interpretive comments" concerning the
basic 1940 *Statement*. These included the following: "Most church-related institutions no longer
need or desire the departure from the principle
of academic freedom implied in the 1940 *Statement,* and we do not now endorse such a departure." Indeed, a speaker at the AAUP's 1987
annual meeting in Los Angeles frankly called
for a reexamination of the religious exemption
contained in the 1940 *Statement*.[9] Certainly the
positions of the Catholic educators we have been
examining in this inquiry strongly imply that
they too could well be among those who believe
"church-related institutions no longer need or
desire" protection from professors who insist on

[9] *Chronicle of Higher Education,* July 1, 1987.

their right to teach in them but are determined to teach or say whatever they please, without regard to the tenets of the sponsoring religious body. This position would also certainly accord with the secularizing trends of the times.

However, it should be pointed out that the 1970 AAUP "interpretive comments" are not endorsed by the same 120 academic and professional associations that endorsed its official 1940 *Statement.* If the later comments are really any more than a feeler or trial balloon, and if the AAUP really wishes to change its position on the traditional exemption accorded to religiously affiliated institutions, it should, in all honesty, reissue its basic *Statement* and seek the same endorsement for it from the academic community that its current *Statement* now enjoys. Until the AAUP does so, we are entitled to continue to consider its 1940 *Statement* as normative and operative.

And this official stated policy of the principal group promoting and defending the academic freedom of faculty members is exactly the *same* policy we earlier saw to be that of the accrediting agencies: religiously affiliated colleges and universities are not guilty of violations of academic freedom if they make clear in advance what restrictions on faculty expression or behavior apply to their institutions. George Keller characterizes the AAUP quite harshly as being "a narrow protective league that guards faculty rights such as academic freedom and tenure rather than [being] an encompassing professional association that insures professional standards, behavior, and obligations and censures or expels members culpable of fraud, abuses of intellectual freedom, incompetency, and gross violations of ethics".[10] Yet even the AAUP has been constrained to recognize that academic freedom is not an absolute, especially where religiously affiliated colleges and universities are concerned.

Nevertheless the AAUP does issue public "censures" of schools held to be in violation of its principles of academic freedom. Usually these "censures" are given to colleges that have failed to respect academic tenure or have dismissed a professor without appropriate due process or something of the sort; sometimes it is the governing board of the institution that is censured. It is not clear from the published Censure List and the kinds of cases discussed that there are many cases where a professor's "freedom of expression" has been muzzled; it appears most often to be a matter of failure to hire or give tenure to a professor who is thought to have abused his academic position, who holds Marxist views, and the like. It is worth looking briefly at this AAUP Censure List.

[10] Keller, *Academic Strategy*, p. 29.

V

Schools "Censured" for
Violations of Academic Freedom

It is worth summarizing some of the cases where the AAUP has censured a college in order to get the flavor of the kinds of things the AAUP gets involved in and to understand the implications of an uncritical acceptance of AAUP standards of academic freedom as the norm and ideal for American academia. For convenience we will briefly summarize four cases where an AAUP censure was imposed in 1987.[1]

In the first of these cases, Husson College in Maine was censured for dismissing a professor who had frequently criticized the college administration. The college claimed that the professor's position was being eliminated because of financial exigencies, but the AAUP claimed to have found that another position in the professor's department had opened up during the same period and was not offered to him in spite of his reported excellent teaching record. The financial exigencies cited by the college were

[1] *Chronicle of Higher Education*, June 17 and July 1, 1987.

therefore not really the reason for the dismissal, according to the AAUP.

Morgan State University, a historically black college in Maryland, was also censured in 1987 for dismissing nineteen tenured faculty members. The university claimed this action had been a part of a retrenchment ordered by the Maryland General Assembly following a significant enrollment decline. The AAUP contended that the legislature had not specifically ordered faculty cuts and that "less drastic means could have been employed"; in a blow against academic snobbery, the AAUP objected particularly to the fact that some nontenured Ph.D.'s had been retained while some tenured non-Ph.D.'s were being dismissed.

The third 1987 case, that of Southern Nazarene University in Oklahoma, involved six professors who were laid off for what the university said were financial reasons. The president of the university subsequently informed the AAUP that moral turpitude had also been involved in some of the dismissals. The AAUP found that academic due process had been denied and that the university's action had "served to besmirch the reputations of the entire group". Apparently violation of "due process" is the principal kind of "moral turpitude" that calls for sanctions these days; other types do not count.

The president of Southern Nazarene declared in an interview that the AAUP's "policies had no relevance to the internal matters of a private, denominational institution". This appears to be an instance that would seem to belie the AAUP "interpretive comment" quoted earlier to the effect that "church-related institutions no longer need or desire the departure from the principle of academic freedom implied in the 1940 *Statement*"—has the AAUP consulted any *churches* about this?

The 1987 AAUP censure case that received the most publicity was one involving the Catholic University of Puerto Rico, which dismissed a tenured faculty member who had remarried after a divorce. The university said that the professor had been informed in advance of being hired of a contractual obligation to remain in good standing with the Catholic Church. A University regulation in fact allows tenured faculty to be dismissed for "professional or personal conduct that violates the moral and doctrinal principles of the Catholic Church". Nevertheless, the AAUP found that since the university did not demonstrate that the professor was "unfit to teach" or that "her continued presence in the classroom posed an immediate danger to herself or to her students" (the AAUP's *own* standards, not the school's), her dismissal was "in outrageous violation of her personal rights and freedoms", meriting "condemnation in the strongest terms".

It is not necessary to agree in any way with the Catholic Church to be aware that the Catholic Church forbids remarriage after divorce; this is common knowledge. Since the professor in question had freely entered into a contractual arrangement that required continued adherence to this and all other "moral and doctrinal principles of the Catholic Church", there would seem to be no grounds for censure at all on the AAUP's own official principles—unless the AAUP is in fact now making the judgment that remarriage after divorce, generally accepted as it is in our society at large, could never be legitimate grounds for dismissal from any position, even within a community that continues to forbid it. To impose an official, public sanction for this—and an AAUP censure is undoubtedly a public sanction—would seem to deny to religious communities who deny remarriage after divorce the right to the free exercise of their religion. Here, finally, is a genuine First Amendment issue! Some of our guardians of that particular Amendment ought to consider taking it up and defending the Catholic University of Puerto Rico against the AAUP!

These four cases, then, give the flavor of the

kinds of censures currently being imposed by
the AAUP. With the addition of these four
schools to the AAUP Censure List in 1987—
actually, six other institutions were *removed* in
1987—the list now contains the names of forty-
seven schools, of which only about seven or eight
can be identified by their names as being defi-
nitely religiously affiliated (only three of these
are Catholic.)[2] This would certainly seem to
suggest that religiously affiliated institutions are
far from the worst offenders against academic
freedom, even in the eyes of the AAUP.

The suggestion that has been made, and that
is under examination here, however, is that the
failure of a school to observe academic freedom
as commonly understood in America could lead
to the loss of government aid, either directly or
through loss of the school's accreditation. I
therefore decided to check the schools on the
current AAUP Censure List against the U.S.
Department of Education's list of institutions
eligible for federal aid. The results obtained
should not be surprising in the light of what has
been brought out in this inquiry up to this point;
it may be surprising to some anyway, in view of
the mythology that continues to surround this
whole subject. The results were these: *all of the*

[2] Ibid., July 1, 1987.

47 institutions on the current AAUP Censure List, without exception, were found to be eligible for federal aid and in fact to be receiving some form of federal aid at the time of this writing. Several of the schools were being closely monitored by the Department of Education because of financial management problems, but all were continuing to receive federal aid.

Evidently it is *not* the normal practice of accrediting agencies to withdraw accreditation when a school is censured by the AAUP for a violation of academic freedom. The AAUP Censure List does *not* constitute the negative standard for academic freedom in America. Censured schools go right on being accredited and go right on receiving federal aid. This seems to be the current actual practice in America. The realization of this must inevitably provide a most pointed and enlightening perspective on the often imagined scenario of, say, a Catholic college deciding to remove a heterodox theology professor only to be faced inexorably, as is thought and widely repeated, with a loss of accreditation and then a loss of federal aid. . . . The entire scenario is fanciful. Not a single instance of anything remotely resembling such a thing can be found in the recent history of higher education in America.

VI

Federal Recognition of Accrediting Agencies

Before we leave the subject of accreditation—the threshold requirement, as we have noted, for the receipt of any type of federal aid to higher education—we must note one final fact about the current federal role in the accreditation process that ought to reassure definitively any religiously affiliated college fearful that some federal "Big Brother" might be trying to make it renounce its religious character as the price of continued federal funding. It is to be hoped that what has been covered up to now will already be sufficiently reassuring. Nevertheless, there is yet another fact that demonstrates that as far as student or institutional financial aid for higher education is concerned, the current federal function is ideologically "blind"; at least in this area the government is not attempting to promote secularism as the price of such aid.

Schools, then, are required to be accredited in order to qualify for eligibility for federal funding for higher education. Accreditation is granted by agencies that are officially private,

63

voluntary agencies not under the control of the
government. Accrediting agencies can be either
institutional, such as the New England Association of Schools and Colleges, which accredits
entire higher education institutions in the New
England states; or specialized, such as the
Council of the Section of Legal Education and
Admissions to the Bar of the American Bar
Association, which accredits law schools nation-
wide.

In order to be able to accredit colleges and
universities for purposes of federal aid, an accrediting agency must be "recognized" by the
Secretary of Education. The law that mandates
this "recognition" by the Secretary requires only
that he publish a list of "the accrediting agencies
and associations which he determines to be reli-
able authorities as to the *quality* of training offered by educational institutions or programs"
(emphasis added).[1] We should again note that
educational *quality,* not anything such as "institutional autonomy" or "academic freedom", is
what is principally at issue in the whole accreditation process.

As we have abundantly seen in the course of

---

[1] See *Nationally Recognized Accrediting Agencies and Associations,* Department of Education, Office of Postsecondary
Education, June 1985, p. 5.

this inquiry, Catholic and other religiously affiliated colleges and universities have been and continue to be regularly accredited by existing accrediting agencies and associations—and hence continue to be eligible for and receive most types of federal aid for higher education.

However, there is a fear that persists among some Catholic and other religiously affiliated higher education institutions. They fear that they might still end up being strangled by the strings attached to federal educational aid. That fear is not entirely fanciful, when we consider how often the blind working of some federal enactment can lead and has led to certain forms of disability and injustice. This has been the case even with the administration of some well-intentioned civil rights laws, for example; we shall look at a possible glaring example of this farther on. Eternal vigilance, in short, is *still* the price of liberty.

Federal aid under the Higher Education Act of 1965, as amended, however, does not currently seem to have any such strings that might strangle. The bigger fear might be that secularization could come to appear such a necessary and inevitable part of the air we breathe that "religious exemptions" could no longer be seen to be justified. We saw the AAUP apparently heading in that very direction, in fact, presum-

ing to judge independently which religious tenets a religious institution might continue to hold
essential. What if accrediting agencies applied
such a "negative religious test" and refused to
accredit schools that insisted on affirming their
religious character?

In an article published in *America* magazine in
February 1987, I suggested the following as a
possible solution in any situation where problems for religious schools should ever arise with
regard to accreditation:

> There remains a simple remedy, one that is
> entirely consistent with our system of private,
> voluntary accreditation. Any groups or classes
> of schools—for example, the 230-odd group of
> Catholic colleges and universities in the United
> States—are entirely free to organize their own
> accrediting agency, just as barber colleges and
> cosmetology or chiropractic schools have their
> own accrediting agencies. If the Catholic col-
> leges and universities were simply to establish
> their own accrediting agency, it is hard to imag-
> ine on what grounds the Secretary of Education
> would fail to "recognize" its accreditation of
> schools for purposes of federal aid, provided it
> maintained the educational standards expected
> of accrediting agencies, as spelled out in the
> Department of Education publication entitled
> "Nationally Recognized Accrediting Agencies
> and Associations".

The establishment of such a specialized agency for the express purpose of accreditation could provide definitive reassurance to those Catholic colleges that apparently fear that their federal aid might possibly be jeopardized or withdrawn if they insist on both their Catholic character and their right under our system to maintain their organic links with the Catholic Church.[2]

The Secretary of Education currently recognizes for accrediting purposes, for example, an Association of Bible Colleges and an Association of Advanced Rabbinical and Talmudic Schools. There is no reason in the world why he could not also recognize an Association of Catholic Colleges and Universities for strictly accrediting purposes. It may not be at all necessary, as the evidence we have examined up to this point suggests; but if it ever is necessary, it is eminently possible—and doable by the Catholic schools themselves.

[2] *America,* Feb. 7, 1987, pp. 98, 112.

VII

Supreme Court Decisions Affecting Religiously Affiliated Colleges and Universities

It is necessary at this point to consider the implications of some recent Supreme Court decisions affecting government aid to higher education. As is well known, the Supreme Court has effectively prohibited nearly every form of government aid to church-affiliated elementary and secondary schools. While the case with regard to higher education is somewhat different, as we have already noted, it is true that there have also been a number of court cases affecting higher education, especially since the 1970s. It is certainly to be feared that, so long as credence is given to the doctrinaire idea that government aid to religiously affiliated schools at any level might somehow constitute an unconstitutional governmental "establishment" of religion, the Supreme Court could always extend this doctrinaire idea to higher education, where it has been applied only to a very limited extent up to now. Moreover, although the Supreme Court does "follow the election returns", the trouble

today is that American society has become so
secularized that public opinion no longer consistently upholds traditional ideas of morality or
religion that were simply assumed at the time the
Constitution was put in place. All too often the
Court's principles just reflect what exists "out
there" in society, and society has moved far from
the idea that there exists a God-given morality
and justice to which even secular laws should
ultimately conform. Rather, man is now considered to be the measure of all things in exactly the
sense the ancient Greek Sophists meant. In this
situation, it is always possible that religiously
affiliated higher education institutions could at
some point be penalized as severely as church-
related elementary and secondary schools have
already been penalized.

At the moment, however, the contrary must
be affirmed. The most recent Supreme Court
decision affecting higher education strongly
supports the constitutional right of a student
studying for the Christian ministry to receive
government aid. In the case of *Witters* v. *Washington Department of Services for the Blind,* handed
down in January 1986,[1] all nine justices of the
Supreme Court agreed unanimously that a
Washington State program for the handicapped

[1] *Chronicle of Higher Education,* Feb. 5, 1986.

supported with both state and federal money could not be denied to a handicapped student studying to be a Christian minister because, in the words of Justice Thurgood Marshall, writing for the Court, "any aid provided under Washington's program that ultimately flows to religious institutions does so only as a result of the genuinely independent and private choices of aid recipients."

Although it is somewhat troubling that the free choice and election of the student recipient are the only basis the Court sees on which a religiously affiliated school might be entitled to public aid, it is entirely consistent with the history of student financial assistance going back to the World War II GI Bill of Rights: students are entitled to it quite independently of the religious character, if any, of the schools they elect to attend.

As has also already been noted, by far the greater amount—over 93 percent—of government aid available to higher education consists of assistance to students rather than direct assistance to institutions as such. A veritable "voucher system", long advocated but never achieved by proponents of Catholic, Christian, Hebrew, and other private schools at the lower levels, exists and flourishes in America at the higher education level. Whatever the degree of danger that the Supreme Court might extend more consistently to higher education the principles in accordance with which it has virtually excluded institutional aid to church-related elementary and secondary schools, there appears to be little or no danger that government assistance to students in religiously affiliated colleges and universities will be jeopardized so long as the assumptions in place for nearly the past half century remain what they are.

It is therefore highly misleading to contend, as did the Association of Catholic Colleges and Universities in its response to the 1985 Roman draft of a document on Catholic Universities, that "thousands of potential students would be unable to use the grants to which they are entitled as citizens at a Catholic college/university".[2] The likelihood that any of these students would lose their entitlement is about as close to zero at the moment as is possible, so long as the schools they attend retain their accreditation— and, as has been amply documented above, the likelihood that these schools would lose their accreditation as long as they maintain quality educational standards is similarly close to zero. The greater part of government aid currently flowing to religiously affiliated colleges in the

[2] See chapter 1, n. 5, above.

form of assistance to the students attending them will in all likelihood continue to flow, even if the Supreme Court does apply its exclusionary principles more strictly to higher education.

Direct institutional aid, however, does represent a somewhat different case. Religiously affiliated schools currently enjoy access to a number of federal and state programs of institutional aid to higher education for purely secular purposes; but under the current Supreme Court interpretations of the First Amendment, their claim to participate is less solid than is the claim of their students to receive financial aid.

In a 1971 case, *Lemon* v. *Kurtzman,* the Supreme Court laid down a three-part test for determining the constitutionality of statutes authorizing government aid to religiously affiliated schools under the establishment clause of the First Amendment. According to this test:

> First, the statute must have a secular legislative purpose; second, its principal or primary effect must be one that neither advances nor inhibits religion . . . ; finally the statute must not foster "an excessive entanglement with religion".[3]

As applied to higher education, the Court held in another case issued at the same time,

[3] *Lemon* v. *Kurtzman,* 430 U.S. 602, 612–13 (1971).

Tilton v. *Richardson,* that, in the case of four church-related institutions of higher education in Connecticut, the degree of "entanglement with religion" was insufficient to prohibit these schools from benefiting from construction grants for secular facilities under the Federal Higher Education Facilities Act of 1963.[4] In fact, religiously affiliated colleges continue to qualify today for federal academic facilities grants and loans, as they do for a variety of other institutional programs, always for purely secular purposes.

The ACCU, however, has conspicuously seized on this Tilton case, in conjunction with a 1976 case, *Roemer* v. *Board of Public Works,* in which some private Catholic colleges were similarly judged not to be pervasively sectarian and hence able to benefit from a Maryland State program of aid to private colleges. According to the ACCU, these two cases constitute the decisive proof that Catholic colleges could lose all government aid if they were ever found to be "controlled" by the Catholic Church. The ACCU quotes the following *obiter dicta* from Roemer:

> Despite their formal affiliation with the Roman Catholic Church, the colleges are "characterized

[4] *Tilton* v. *Richardson,* 430 U.S. 672 (1971).

by a high degree of institutional autonomy".
None of the four receives funds from or makes
reports to the Catholic Church. The church is
represented on their governing boards, but . . .
"no instance of church considerations into college decisions was shown."[5]

"It is clear", the ACCU concludes, "that the
favorable decisions regarding public aid to
Catholic colleges or universities are founded on
a perception by the court that the church does
not control them."[6]

This is not necessarily so. That particular
conclusion depends on what is meant by "control". Most religiously affiliated institutions—a
fact already touched on in the discussion of
accreditation—are indeed "characterized by a
high degree of institutional autonomy" in the
sense that, as institutions of higher learning,
they are separate and distinct from the churches
that sponsor them, just as state colleges and
universities are separate and distinct from state
authorities that sponsor *them*.

Moreover, the importance of a college education to older students, even when carried out
within the framework of a particular religion, is
and always has been understood to be some-

[5] *Roemer v. Board of Public Works*, 426 U.S. 736 (1976).
[6] See chapter 1, n. 5, above.

thing that goes far beyond mere "indoctrination" in, say, the various articles of a catechism; a certain degree of mature, religious commitment on the part of most students can be inferred from their very presence on that particular kind of campus.

The idea that there is no middle ground between considering colleges sponsored by a church, such as parochial schools, to be "an arm of the church", as Father Theodore M. Hesburgh apparently does, and considering only colleges that are totally free, independent, and autonomous to be institutions of higher learning in the true sense, is a simplification that bears little relation to the reality of higher education in the United States, past or present.

Even colleges "characterized by a high degree of institutional autonomy", as is encouraged (but not strictly required) by the accrediting agencies, are not always and necessarily independent of *any* oversight or "control" on the part of their sponsoring bodies, whether church or state or other sponsoring body; on the contrary, some degree of dependence is probably the norm; it is a matter of degree. With regard to those Catholic colleges that seem to be so fearful of the consequences of invoking Canon 812 of the Church's Code of Canon Law, it should be recalled that this canon is concerned only with "those who teach theological subjects", not with the institution's autonomy as a whole. Surely, this constitutes legitimate oversight in the case of a religiously affiliated school.

Nor do colleges necessarily have to receive money directly from their sponsors in order to be subordinate and subject to them in a sense such as being answerable to them in the type of theology they teach. It is probably broadly true, though, that religiously affiliated institutions are financially dependent on the contributions of the *communities* adhering to their sponsoring churches. This makes it all the more important, as a matter of "truth in advertising", that they are what they claim to be in a sense that their sponsoring churches have a perfect right to define for them.

Finally, neither the accrediting agencies nor the Supreme Court, as evidenced by the *Roemer* case, seem to object to sponsoring church representation on college governing boards. Yet such representation is normally all that a church might require to ensure that a school it sponsors remains authentic from the point of view, for example, of the theology taught there.

Thus, the *Roemer* case proves a good deal less than is claimed for it. A school could meet all the Court criteria quoted above without abandoning a true religious character, properly understood. It is surely theoretically possible to teach within an authentic religious tradition without being "pervasively sectarian" in the sense meant by the Court. In point of fact, scores of religiously affiliated institutions do continue to benefit from various government institutional aid programs at the same time that they both teach within a faith-oriented framework and are also subject to varying degrees of outside oversight and "control". It is no doubt true that the doctrine enshrined in decisions such as *Roemer* represents a potential threat to such institutions, perhaps a serious threat. It is probably equally true that the principles assumed in *Roemer* and similar cases that invoke the "wall of separation" between church and state evidence an abiding secularism hostile to religiously affiliated schools—as if no work carried out in the name of religion could ever possibly serve the common good. Nevertheless, *Roemer* is far from representing an irreversible fait accompli at the present time.

Indeed, cases such as *Roemer* cannot possibly be considered the last word on the subject. Where such decisions encroach, actually or potentially, on authentic rights, including the rights of religious bodies to operate their own colleges and the rights of parents and students to select such religiously affiliated colleges, the reversal of these Court decisions must be actively sought through legal challenges. Where would education for blacks be today if the 1896 Supreme Court case *Plessy* v. *Ferguson* sanctioning the doctrine of "separate but equal" in educational and other public facilities had simply been accepted as the last word on the subject? That pernicious doctrine obtained for more than half a century—*Roemer* and *Tilton,* by contrast, have only been in place since the 1970s.

Plessy was finally reversed by *Brown* v. *Topeka Board of Education* in 1954, which required school districts to move toward integration "with all deliberate speed". However, *Brown* only came about because the black community (with the moral support of probably a majority of Americans), refused to accept second-class, so-called separate but equal status; and, by persisting, blacks eventually managed to get *Plessy* reversed. This in no way means that the educational problems of blacks were all suddenly solved, but it does demonstrate that a determined minority sure of its aims can successfully work within the free American political and judicial system to remedy manifest abuses where they exist.

One of the manifest abuses that exists at the present time is, of course, the second-class status currently accorded to church-related, synagogue-related, and no doubt even mosque-related schools in this country, especially at the lower levels. Taxes are required from everybody for the support of the public schools, and nobody disputes the justice of this. It is not clear that justice is equally served, however, when taxpayers who elect private schools must pay double to receive few or no public benefits, especially when the private schools they elect so plainly do serve the common good (as for example, in the demonstrable contributions that inner-city Catholic schools are currently making to the education of minority children, many of them not Catholics). The late Father John Courtney Murray, S.J., described the situation succinctly nearly thirty years ago:

> The doctrine that public aid should be denied by law to certain schools simply on the grounds that they teach a particular religion was never in conformity with the moral canon of distributive justice. This moral norm requires that government, in distributing burdens and benefits within the community, should have in view the needs, merits, and capacities of the various groups of citizens and society in general. The operation of this norm is visible in many fields—income tax laws, selective service, social security, labor laws, etc. It ought likewise to control the action of government in support of schools. The

principle of distributive justice would require
that a proportionately just measure of public
support should be available to such schools as
serve the public cause of popular education,
whether these schools be specifically religious in
their affiliation and orientation, or not.[7]

The situation described by Father Murray has
not changed.[8] Indeed, as the *Tilton* and *Roemer*
cases themselves demonstrate, the kind of think-
ing that has denied government aid to religiously affiliated schools could also be applied
more strictly to higher education. The proper
response to this state of affairs, though, is not to
claim that religiously affiliated colleges, therefore, must be "independent" of and cannot in
any way be "controlled" by their church sponsors; the proper response is to challenge this
kind of discrimination through the legal and
political channels available to American citizens.
The legitimate "control" and oversight that

[7] John Courtney Murray, S.J., *We Hold These Truths:
Catholic Reflections on the America Proposition* (New York:
Sheed and Ward, 1960), p. 146.

[8] For a recent account of how a prejudiced refusal to
admit the justice of allowing Catholic or other private
school students to benefit from federal aid to education
delayed such federal aid for many years, see Ravitch,
Troubled Crusade, pp. 26–42.

church authorities have a right to exercise over the colleges they sponsor, just as state legislators exercise similar oversight and "control" over the colleges they sponsor, is in no intelligible sense an "establishment of religion". The very idea is absurd, even if, for the moment, it unfortunately happens to be enshrined in Supreme Court case law. The fathers of the Constitution, at a time when the American higher education enterprise of the day was almost entirely in religious hands, would have rubbed their eyes in disbelief if anyone had remotely suggested the notion to them.

The First Amendment not only forbids "the establishment of religion"; it also forbids laws prohibiting the "free exercise" thereof. To deny to churches, parents, and students benefits to which all citizens ought to be entitled impartially merely because these churches, parents, and students want an education within a total religious context, is precisely to forbid to them the free exercise of their religion in the full sense of the word. It is a violation of the religious freedom that is supposed to be guaranteed by the Constitution. Rather than acquiescing for fear they might lose some of the benefits they currently enjoy, educators in religiously affiliated colleges, as well as their sponsoring churches and communities, ought to be standing up for these principles. They have every right to do so; they also have a responsibility to do so.

The president of the Christian College Coalition, an organization of some seventy-two Evangelical colleges, has aptly described the kind of institution that religiously affiliated colleges ought and have a right to be:

> The stand of our schools is, if you're earnest about your faith, you can't compartmentalize it. It weaves through everything you do . . . the issue involved is a very basic, fundamental issue that applies to any faith-related college.[9]

It should be clear from what has been brought out in this inquiry that nothing in the American system of higher education should preclude the operation of schools of this type, although the right to continue to do so no doubt has to be fought for in the face of some of the secularizing trends of today, especially those that have such undue influence over the Supreme Court with regard to First Amendment issues. As Pope John Paul II recently said in an address at the Catholic University of Lyons in France:

> The purpose of a Catholic university lies in the pursuit of research and instruction [but] such a university must likewise allow the students to

[9] *Chronicle of Higher Education,* Nov. 27, 1985.

carry on their studies in an atmosphere consistent with the faith, to find the means to deepen this faith, to learn the rudiments of the spiritual life and Christian activity. . . . Such a demand concerns first of all the professors of the staff who must not be afraid of bearing witness to the faith which motivates them, to their ethical reflection in the light of the Church's teaching. Thus will youth be led freely to choose the path of the gospel in the midst of the profusion of ideologies and standards of behavior of our times.[10]

The pontiff's vision of what a Catholic university ought to be is in no way incompatible with established American practice in higher education.

[10] Pope John Paul II, "Remarks to a Group from the Catholic University of Lyons", *L'Osservatore Romano* (weekly edition in English), Mar. 23, 1987.

VIII

A Glance at State Aid to Religiously Affiliated Institutions

Up to this point, the emphasis has been placed almost entirely on federal aid to higher education. To some extent the states represent a different case. Unlike the federal government, the states legislate specific requirements for the operation of higher education institutions; furthermore, although the greater part of government aid is federal, many states also have their own programs of aid from which both private colleges and universities and the students attending them can sometimes benefit.

In touching on the question of state aid to private colleges at all, though, we should be aware that the amounts of state aid of all kinds flowing to private colleges is very small, compared not only to the much larger amounts of federal aid that private colleges normally receive, but, especially, to what they receive in tuitions and fees and from private sources. The issue of state aid can almost nowhere be considered decisive for private colleges.

Private colleges on the average derive only 1.4

percent of their income from money appropriated directly by the states or localities in which they are located; they get another 2.2 percent of their income in grants and contracts from those same states and localities. By contrast they derive almost 15 percent of their income from federal aid. As we noted at the outset, federal aid is thus considerably more important than state aid. Even then, private colleges and universities still derive more than 70 percent of their income from tuition, fees, endowments, and the like, so that there remains at least a question about whether all types of government aid together really constitute an absolutely critical factor for private colleges and universities.[1] A few colleges, apparently, do without it entirely.

It is true, however, that state requirements regarding religiously affiliated schools can sometimes be more stringent than the federal requirements that have been under review in this inquiry. In Washington State, for example, it is not just a matter of court interpretations that attach certain disabilities to religiously affiliated colleges in the matter of financial aid. The Washington State Constitution itself stipulates that

[1] *The Condition of Education,* 1986 edition (Center for Education Statistics, U.S. Department of Education), pp. 110–11.

"no public money or property shall be appropriated for or applied to any religious worship, exercise or instruction, or the support of any religious establishment" (Article I, 11); and that "all schools maintained or supported wholly or in part by the public funds shall be forever free from sectarian control or influence" (Article IX, 4).[2]

Similarly, the New York State Constitution prohibits any aid to religious schools. Around twenty years ago, when New York State's so-called Bundy Funds became available to higher education, a number of then-Catholic colleges and universities proceeded to convert themselves into legally independent, nondenominational, and nonsectarian institutions in order to be eligible to receive this state aid. This proved to be the beginning of a trend; many schools have followed suit since. Monsignor Michael J. Wrenn, relying on a book-length study of Fordham University's transformation from a Catholic Jesuit institution into an officially secular one, has chronicled the results as far as New York is concerned, both for Fordham and for a number of other erstwhile Catholic institutions.[3] Ac-

[2] Quoted in *Witters v. Washington Department of Services for the Blind,* in *Chronicle of Higher Education,* Feb. 5, 1986.

[3] Rev. Msgr. Michael J. Wrenn, "'Catholic' Universities:

cording to Monsignor Wrenn's account, legal advice provided to Fordham about what it would have to do to qualify for the available state aid was, quite simply, "to demonstrate that it was in fact not a religious school". The university elected to follow this legal advice, thereby blazing a trail for other institutions that have followed since; and the university so informed the New York State Department of Education in July 1968: "Fordham University now . . . elects to be considered as a nondenominational institution for the purposes of Section 313 of the Education Law."

One trouble with this kind of solution, of course, is that the institution's status remains unclear in the public mind. Nearly twenty years after Fordham officially decided to become "nondenominational . . . for the purposes of . . . the Education Law", the current president of Fordham, Father Joseph A. O'Hare, S.J., is quoted as complaining that the university would face "morale and identity problems" if it were ever asked by the archbishop of New York to

---

Independent or Nonsectarian?" *Fidelity,* Mar. 1987, pp. 13–15. Msgr. Wrenn bases his comments mostly on Walter Gellhous and R. Kent Greenawalt, *The Sectarian College and the Public Purse* (Dobbs Ferry, N.Y.: Oceana Publications, 1970).

cease calling itself "Catholic" in accordance with the proposed new pontifical document on Catholic universities.[4] Apparently Fordham has continued, if not to call itself Catholic in any legal sense, at least not to protest too loudly if parents, students, alumni, and others within the Catholic community on whom the institution no doubt continues to depend for a large measure of its support go on believing that an institution founded and still heavily staffed by Jesuits remains in some sense "Catholic". In the news story just quoted, Father O'Hare further defines a Catholic university as requiring merely a "critical mass of intelligent and dedicated Catholics" to be present on its campus. Thus, there must be at least a sense in which even Father O'Hare believes Fordham continues to be "Catholic" in spite of its official secular legal status.

The same thing is true, apparently, of many of the members of the Association of Catholic Colleges and Universities. Surely they are claiming to be "Catholic", at least in some sense, by their very membership in an organization of that name. And they apparently believe that they have a perfect right to protest when the Catholic Church seems to be in the process of defining

[4] "Shortsighted: Fordham President Criticizes Vatican Proposals", *Catholic New York*, Oct. 30, 1986.

more strictly than they do what a Catholic university should be. At the same time, in the words of the ACCU Executive Director, Sister Alice Gallin, O.S.U., these colleges "are insisting on freedom from external control by either state or church".[5]

An outside observer would be tempted to conclude from all this that Catholic colleges cannot necessarily have it both ways. If they elect to become purely secular institutions in order, as they apparently believe or at least publicly state, to be able to qualify for financial aid from radically secularizing courts or state governments, then it would not seem at all unfair to an impartial observer if their "former" sponsoring Church were publicly to declare them to be what they have in fact elected to be, that is, no longer "Catholic".

In point of fact, the rush to secularize was surely never justified in the first place in the case of schools of this type. It is clear from what has been brought out in this inquiry that Catholic colleges were never in serious danger of losing the bulk of the federal aid they currently enjoy, even while retaining full affiliation with the

[5] Alice Gallin, O.S.U., letter to the editor, *America*, Apr. 4, 1987, p. 292.

Catholic Church. If requirements have been somewhat stricter in some states, such as New York—a review of the requirements in all the fifty states is beyond the scope of the present inquiry—this no doubt has posed a separate problem for some schools. Yet, as we have seen, the amounts of state aid available cannot have been decisive in very many cases.

Moreover, the fact remains that the freedom of the American political and judicial systems, at the state as well as at the federal levels, has at no point been suspended; religiously affiliated institutions unjustly precluded by their religious character from receiving public aid intended for all have always had and still have every right to secure the redress of their grievances through the political and judicial means available to all Americans. The Catholic community remains by far the largest "minority" in the United States. It is fair to say that no public policy opposed with cogent and persuasive reasons by a united Catholic community both knowledgeable and determined about its rights and responsibilities could long survive in the United States. Once again, one has to wonder where American blacks, far fewer in numbers than Catholics, would be today if they had simply continued to acquiesce in the various kinds of disabilities that a number of courts and state governments had tried to impose on them.

More than that, to acquiesce in such patently unjust disabilities is to contribute to the possible forfeiture of rights that belong to all citizens. Nobody has the right to pursue narrow financial self-interest against the rights and responsibilities that are essential to the functioning of a democratic political and judicial system. Rather, there is a duty to work for the justice that the American system claims to offer to all impartially. If it is really true that religiously affiliated colleges are in danger of losing the benefits they enjoy because a hostile government, possibly at the urging of the American Civil Liberties Union, Americans United for the Separation of Church and State, or other secularizing groups, stands ready to penalize them further because of their religious character, then it is not even good strategy simply to acquiesce in the disabilities inherent in current court interpretations of church-state issues. A more aggressive strategy that actively seeks to secure one's rights is surely called for, if only on the theory that the best defense is to take the offense. Such a strategy would be totally in keeping with the way politics is regularly practiced in the United States by just about everybody.

Finally, as the Washington State case cited above amply proves, even repressive state constitutional and other legal constraints are ultimately subject to federal precedents. Many accept the truth of what Justice Byron R. White has said, that the Supreme Court's "decisions finding constitutional violations where a state provides aid to private schools or their students misconstrue the Establishment Clause and disserve the public interest"[6]—and it is a thesis of this inquiry that the truth of this proposition is self-evident. At least as serious an effort needs to be made to influence the federal judiciary to return to the canons of truth and justice on which this country was founded as has so successfully been made up to now by the radical secularists in the opposite direction—and as serious an effort as has been continually made by schools of all types to lobby for more federal aid. The Constitution is supposed to guarantee the "free exercise" of religion in addition to forbidding any "establishment" of it. As Chief Justice Rehnquist has written, speaking about the famous supposed "wall of separation" between church and state:

[6] Opinion in *Witters* v. *Washington Department of Services for the Blind* (see n. 2 above).

The greatest injury of the "wall" notion is its mischievous diversion of judges from the actual intentions of the drafters of the Bill of Rights. The "crucible of litigation" is well adapted to adjudicating factual disputes on the basis of testimony presented in court, but no amount of repetition of historical errors in judicial opinions can make the errors true. The "wall of separation between church and State" is a metaphor based on bad history, a metaphor which has proven useless as a guide to judging. It should be frankly and explicitly abandoned.[7]

[7] Justice William H. Rehnquist, in *Wallace* v. *Jaffee* (1985). Quoted in Charles J. Cooper and Nelson Lund, "Landmarks of Constitutional Interpretation", *Policy Review*, Spring 1987, no. 40, p. 23.

IX

The Real Threat to
"Institutional Autonomy"

Continued acquiescence in current secularizing trends for perceived short-term financial advantage works to the distinct disadvantage of the basic character of religiously affiliated colleges and universities. A dramatic example of this came out in the consideration and approval by a Senate committee of the so-named Civil Rights Restoration Act of 1987 by the U.S. Senate in the spring of 1987. The CRRA was a piece of legislation intended to restore the enforcement power of federal civil rights laws, which had been lost when the U.S. Supreme Court decided in a 1984 case that discrimination in educational programs benefiting from federal aid applied only to the specific programs in question and not to the entire college or university in which the programs were located. In *Grove City College* v. *Bell*,[1] the Supreme Court ruled that Title IX of a law known as the Education Amendments of 1972, which forbids discrimination on the basis

---

[1] *Grove City* v. *Bell*, 465 U.S. 555 (1984).

of sex in federally assisted education programs, did not apply to the situation of Grove City College in Pennsylvania, a small liberal arts college that had historically refused on principle all direct federal institutional aid. However, a small number of its students were receiving federal Basic Educational Opportunity Grants, and the question was, when the college was held to be discriminating against women in its athletic programs, whether the prohibition against discrimination applied to the institution across the board or merely to the athletic programs themselves (which, of course, were *not* directly federally funded). The Court ruled in favor of the latter proposition, and the result was that the federal government could not cut off the financial aid going to Grove City College students since this aid was in no way connected to the athletic programs found to be discriminating against women.

The decision in this case affected the enforcement of civil rights legislation across the board. Title IX prohibited discrimination on the basis of sex; discrimination on the basis of age, handicap, or race is similarly prohibited by other special civil rights laws. Once the principle had been established that the government can cut off aid only to these specific federally funded programs actually found to be practicing discrimination, however, the principle was quickly seen to apply to discrimination of any type, not just to discrimination on the basis of sex.

Before *Grove City,* a school found to be discriminating generally, and not just in a specific federally funded educational program, could always be referred to the Justice Department, which could file suit against the school—the Justice Department, or private parties for that matter, can always file suit against institutions alleged to be in violation of civil rights laws even if they are *not* receiving any federal or state aid, but it is not really very likely that anyone would ever do so in the absence of a government aid issue. After the *Grove City* decision was handed down, however, the government not only could do nothing directly but cut off aid only to the specific programs found to be discriminatory; it could not even look at the other activities of the school not being specifically aided with federal funds.

It was to remedy this state of affairs, intolerable from his point of view, that Senator Edward M. Kennedy (D. Mass.) introduced the Civil Rights Restoration Act of 1987. The CRRA appeared to many to be a rather far-reaching remedy, however, since it proposed to apply the full panoply of civil rights rules and regulations to "all of the operations" of any "entity" benefiting from federal assistance.[2] Specifically, the CRRA was intended to amend four basic civil rights statutes to restore the federal government's power to enforce them across entire institutions: Title IX of the Education Amendments of 1972, Section 504 of the Rehabilitation Act of 1973, the Age Discrimination Act of 1975, and Title VI of the Civil Rights Act of 1964.[3]

Some observers feared that the sweep of the bill's language was so broad that a grocery store accepting federal food stamps or a pharmacy filling a Medicaid prescription would be covered by it.[4] Furthermore, one of the other effects of the original Title IX legislation had been that schools and colleges, with respect to the health benefits provided to their students and employees, were required to treat all pregnancy-related conditions, including "terminations of pregnancy", as "covered". Since abortion is con-

[2] For a reasonably complete account of the whole debate on *Grove City v. Bell* in the U.S. Senate in the spring of 1987, see the stories that appeared in *Education Daily* for Mar. 18, Mar. 23, and Apr. 2, 1987.

[3] "ACE Urges Passage of Civil Rights Restoration Act", *Higher Education and National Affairs*, Apr. 6, 1987.

[4] James J. Kilpatrick, "Stop Yelling about Grove City", *Washington Post*, Mar. 31, 1987.

sidered in current U.S. law as not merely an accepted medical procedure but as a positive "civil right"—courtesy, again, of the U.S. Supreme Court—this requirement that abortion be considered just another "covered" health benefit no doubt possessed a certain weird logic; however that may be, the 1975 federal regulations implementing Title IX adopted it.

There was an exception, however. The requirement to provide abortion coverage did not apply to colleges "controlled by a religious organization", since Congress had written a Section 901(3) into Title IX exempting such religious institutions from any provisions of the act to the extent that their "application would not be consistent with the religious tenets of such organization".

But the broad language of the new Civil Rights Restoration Act threatened to nullify this religious "exception". Part of the drama of the debate over the CRRA that took place in the U.S. Senate in the spring of 1987 lay in the contention by opponents of the CRRA that the bill's strong language applying all federal civil rights regulations to institutions across the board would not only eliminate the "exception" for religiously affiliated colleges; it would actually extend the mandatory abortion requirement to hundreds of teaching hospitals that had not been previously subject to the provisions of Title IX.

Many supporters of civil rights were thus constrained to oppose the CRRA. The United States Catholic Conference, for example, which has been a consistent long-term supporter of civil rights legislation, was obliged to oppose the CRRA unless amended not merely to protect "institutions directly controlled by religious bodies" from having to provide abortions under Title IX, but also, significantly, to protect "institutions which are not directly controlled by a church but are still religious in nature, such as independent religious hospitals or educational centers".[5]

Or: Catholic colleges that have legally secularized themselves, claiming all the while they could lose all their government aid if ever shown to be "controlled" by their sponsoring Church. That claim has been shown to be highly exaggerated, if not quite simply false, but there can be no doubt that a very real danger does threaten these institutions now: the danger that since they are *not* religious organizations "controlled" by their Church, they can now be required to pro-

[5] "Civil Rights Bill Must Be Anti-Abortion, says USCC", *Catholic Herald* (Arlington, Va.), Feb. 26, 1987.

vide abortions against the tenets of their Faith in fulfillment of this kind of civil rights legislation. The "control" by their Church that these schools feared was going to put them in jeopardy with the U.S. government turns out to be the very thing that could have shielded them from the raw power of the U.S. government enforcing a civil rights act. Like the accreditation agencies and the AAUP, Title IX recognized a religious exemption; it did not recognize a secular one. Having given up their formal and legal religious status in order, as they professed to believe, to ensure that the flow of financial aid would continue, these Catholic colleges and universities now face a clear and present danger that they might begin to be *treated* as the wholly secular entities they elected to be. This is a very serious matter, and it has been treated as such. Not only has the U.S. Catholic Conference strenuously tried to seek an exemption for these schools that are no longer "controlled" by the Catholic Church, but merely "affiliated" with it in some largely undefined sense; the principal higher education association in the United States, the American Council on Education (ACE), has also felt obliged to seek an exemption for these same schools. In a letter to Senator Kennedy, the ACE described the problem as "unique to the independent sector of higher education", pointing out how many colleges "deeply committed to religious belief would not qualify for a religious exemption because they are not formally controlled by a religious organization". The National Association of Independent Colleges and Universities (NAICU) was similarly concerned and presented its own testimony to Senator Kennedy's committee.[6]

The trend to secularize on the part of Catholic colleges and universities has thus been fraught with previously unimagined difficulties. The need for "institutional autonomy" and "academic freedom" to qualify for federal aid turns out to be largely a myth, while a very real danger arises precisely for those religious schools that are *not* "controlled" by their sponsoring churches. No doubt few of these schools bargained for anything like this when they decided to secularize themselves and allowed themselves to be governed by wholly independent lay boards, but the debate over the CRRA points to the acute difficulty they may now face of no longer being able to have it both ways, no longer being able to be both "Catholic" for the purpose of attracting students and at the same time totally independent of the Catholic Church for the declared purpose of receiving government aid.

[6] See n. 3 above.

One legislator whose record evidences a particular zeal for mandating "abortion rights", Rep. Patricia Schroeder (D. Colo.), declared on National Public Radio in March 1986 that schools such as Notre Dame and Georgetown are no longer entitled to claim an exemption on religious grounds from providing whatever the law currently views as an established civil right. "I think both Georgetown and Notre Dame have really moved over that line and said, 'We are now secular' ", Representative Schroeder is quoted as having said.[7] There is no reason to believe she is not a harbinger of more of the same to come for erstwhile religious schools. It almost inevitably reminds one of a saying of Georges Clemenceau: "Render into Caesar the things that are Caesar's—and everything is Caesar's."

[7] Quoted in National Right to Life Factsheet, "The 'Civil Rights Restoration Act'—How It Would Force Hospitals and Colleges to Provide Abortion", Feb. 26, 1987. (NRLC, 419 7th Street NW, Washington, D.C. 20004).

X

The Land O'Lakes Statement

What is the real motive and origin of the claim that Catholic colleges and universities must have "institutional autonomy" and "academic freedom"? This inquiry has demonstrated that these things are not strict requirements of the federal or state governments, of the accrediting agencies, or even of the AAUP. On the contrary, the American system of higher education specifically allows for limitations on academic freedom for religious reasons, as it allows an effective measure of institutional control by religious or other sponsoring bodies over the colleges and universities they sponsor. Colleges and universities generally claim "institutional autonomy" and "academic freedom", of course, and in a very large sense rightly so, although actual American practice suggests that these things are in no way considered absolutes even for the large secular universities; hardly any schools have ever attempted to invoke them against the imperatives of U.S. civil rights legislation, for example. Yet even with regard to civil rights legislation, Congress sometimes appears to be more respectful of the competing rights of educational institutions when they are frankly religious than when they are not, as we saw with Title IX. However that may be—and even if it is granted that Catholic educators could not have been expected to foresee the kinds of disabilities that legislation such as the CRRA could impose on them once they could no longer claim religious exemption—it is hard to understand why these institutions have insisted so strongly that they must have "institutional autonomy" and "academic freedom".

Is it really so onerous for an institution claiming "affiliation" with a church—and thus enjoying the benefits of support from that church's *community*—to have to allow the church in question to be able to specify whether the institution is meeting the church's requirements for affiliation, especially with regard to the fairly narrow question of the teaching of theological subjects? As far as Catholic colleges and universities are concerned, the evidence examined in this inquiry suggests that these colleges first decided they wanted to have "institutional autonomy" and "academic freedom"—and only then decided to adduce supposed government requirements for giving out aid as the principal reason they needed to have these two things. Surely those who have worked in higher education should have been the first to know that the

government has never imposed this kind of a
negative religious test for the receipt of student
financial assistance—by far the larger category
of government aid—as has been repeatedly
made clear—and that even if the situation is
more precarious with respect to institutional aid
owing to doctrinaire and one-sided Court interpretations of the First Amendment, there is
again no absolute requirement for "institutional
autonomy" and "academic freedom" before religiously affiliated schools can be eligible for such
aid. And we are in any case talking about no
more than 7 percent of all federal aid in the case
of the latter. Thus the real reason that these
things have been demanded in such categorical
terms by the Currans, Gallins, and Hesburghs
seems to be related to something else besides
government aid.

It would not be within the competence of a
public official to speculate about what that
"something else" might possibly be; the principal purpose of this inquiry has been to try to
ascertain what the conditions and requirements
for government aid actually are with respect to
the widely reiterated but erroneous claim of
some Catholic educators that those conditions
and requirements amount to "institutional autonomy" and "academic freedom". Since it has
been clearly shown that these are *not* the govern-

ment's conditions and requirements in the sense claimed, it remains only to show where the insistence on having them originated.

Perhaps the most significant milestone statement on higher education made by American leaders in Catholic higher education in the postwar era (and, in the Catholic context, in the post–Vatican II era) came in 1967 when twenty-six Catholic educational leaders, including presidents and representatives of the major institutions, issued the so-named Land O'Lakes Statement on "The Nature of the Contemporary Catholic University". This Land O'Lakes Statement lays out exactly where these particular Catholic educators thought they should be, and this quite without regard to the issue of government aid. The statement declares:

> The Catholic university today must be a university in the modern sense of the word, with a strong commitment to and concern for academic excellence. To perform its teaching and research functions effectively, the Catholic university must have a true autonomy and academic freedom in the face of authority of whatever kind, lay or clerical, external to the academic community itself. To say this is simply to assert that *institutional autonomy* and *academic freedom* are essential conditions of life and growth and

indeed of survival for Catholic universities as for all universities [emphasis added].[1]

This "declaration of independence" produced in 1967 by Catholic educators themselves, then, rather than any court decisions or state or federal requirements, seems to be the most likely source for the preoccupation with the questions of "institutional autonomy" and "academic freedom". The whole issue of government aid seems to have been raised later—as if the categorical claims of the Land O'Lakes Statement were not quite as self-evident as they were originally presented as being. Certainly the purely secular institutions that could claim the degree of "institutional autonomy" and "academic freedom" demanded for Catholic institutions in the Land O'Lakes Statement would seem to be rather few and far between—based on the kind of evidence that we have been examining in this inquiry, and as in fact became very clear in the ultimately hardened responses of some secular universities to continuing campus turmoil in the 1970s.

In 1967, after all, at the time of the Land O'Lakes Statement, the call for various kinds of

[1] Quoted in Charles E. Curran and Richard A. McCormick, S.J., eds., *Readings in Moral Theology No. 3: The Magisterium and Morality* (New York: Paulist Press, 1982), p. 394.

freedom and autonomy were well nigh univer-
sal; and society as a whole had scarcely had the
opportunity to measure the effects of it all. It will
be recalled how weak and vacillating were the
responses of many institutions, especially colleges and universities, to the first cries of "up
against the wall!"—especially when "rights" of
any kind were invoked. But as the nihilism and
destructiveness of the campus protests of the
1960s became more evident, the attitudes of
both schools and society at large quite correctly
became much more critical of this kind of activity—and both schools and society at large
began acting more firmly in the face of challenges.

By contrast, the Land O'Lakes Statement
seems to be stuck somewhere back in the sixties.
The Statement upholds the claimed rights of
scholars even while it seems to prescind entirely
from whatever rights and voice Catholic parents, students, the Catholic Church—and, indeed, society at large—might have in a higher
education enterprise that apparently wants to
continue to call itself "Catholic", even as it
presses its case for an unreal freedom and autonomy for faculty and individual institutions.

The Land O'Lakes Statement, then, unre-
alistically sees higher education almost entirely
from the viewpoint of the individual research

professor; it also conveniently exempts the administration from even questioning anything a professor might choose to do. All this is surely a serious distortion of the whole higher education enterprise, and would clearly be such even in the case of completely secular institutions. Surely the model is even less pertinent to the average small Catholic-affiliated liberal arts college. The leaders of Catholic higher education, in short, seem to have adopted a secularist model against their own best long-term interests and those of their schools and constituents. Unfortunately, their decision also contributes little toward the maintenance of the free and pluralistic system of higher education that through many trials and challenges has continued to obtain in the United States and has been described in this inquiry. A return by these Catholic colleges and universities to the authentic system of higher education as practiced in America is "a consummation devoutly to be wished".

XI

Conclusions

It may be fitting to conclude this inquiry by formulating a number of conclusions—both of fact and of value:

— Churches or similar bodies or communities have a moral and legal right under the American system to establish their own colleges and universities and to exercise over them the degree of control necessary to ensure that they authentically embody the tenets and values of their sponsors.

— "Institutional autonomy" and "academic freedom" represent important values in American higher education, but they are not absolute. They do not protect the faculty member alone against the legitimate claims of the institution or protect the institution alone against the legitimate claims of its sponsoring body or society at large.

— Religiously affiliated colleges and universities can legitimately require standards of faith and conduct from their faculty and employees and students so long as these standards are clearly stated in advance and not imposed ex post facto.

— Educational quality is not necessarily or automatically diminished just because a school insists that its instruction be imparted in accordance with the tenets of a religious faith.

— Government aid available to institutions of higher education generally ought to be available also to such of these institutions as are religiously affiliated to the extent that these institutions serve the common good.

— Available government student financial assistance rightly flows to all students in accredited and eligible colleges and universities, regardless of the religious character or lack of it at the schools they are attending.

— It is reasonable for the federal government to continue to require schools to be accredited as a condition of receiving any aid, provided the accrediting process continues to emphasize the quality of education offered and does not attempt to impose requirements on schools that would violate their religious tenets or practices.

— It is not a reasonable interpretation of the First Amendment to maintain that a quality education serving the common good, but imparted within the total context of a faith or religious system, in any sense constitutes a forbidden "establishment of religion" if assisted in any way by the government.

— Restrictions on government educational aid generally available imposed by courts or legislatures based on claims of "an establishment of religion" should be opposed through the political and judicial means available in a free society.

— Short-term financial advantage should not be sought by schools at the cost of condoning injustice; rather, the rights and religious freedom of all should be upheld on principle.

— Religiously affiliated colleges should be prepared to forego government aid entirely rather than acquiesce in any restriction on their First Amendment right to the free exercise of their religion imposed through any court decision, legislative enactment, or government regulatory action.

— Violations of the First Amendment's guarantee of the free exercise of religion are no less violations even if they are imposed by the government in the name of "civil rights" or under civil rights statutes or auspices.